The landscape of the Lancashire spinning districts is unlike any other in Britain. The huge flat-topped brick mills with their square towers (built to house the dust-extraction equipment) and their tall circular chimneys dwarf all other buildings. They are particularly impressive when lit up at night. This aerial photograph was taken of the aptly named Mills Hill district of Middleton in 1935.

THE COTTON INDUSTRY

Chris Aspin

Shire Publications Ltd

CONTENTS

The rise and fall of the cotton industry 3
Preparing the raw cotton 5
Spinning 9
Weaving 19
Finishing the cloth 23
Cotton's impact on the world 26
Social consequences 29
Further reading 32
Places to visit 32

Published by Shire Publications Ltd, Midland House, West Way, Botley, Oxford OX2 0PH, UK. (Website: www.shirebooks.co.uk)
Copyright © 1981 by Chris Aspin. First published 1981; reprinted 1984, 1987, 1991, 1995, 2000, 2004 and 2010. Transferred to digital print on demand 2012.
Shire Library 63. ISBN-13: 978 0 85263 545 2.

Printed in Great Britain by PrintOnDemand-Worldwide.com, Peterborough, UK.

ACKNOWLEDGEMENTS
Illustrations are acknowledged as follows: Burnley Library, page 22 (bottom); Middleton Library, page 1; City of Ghent, page 13; Shirley Institute, page 15 (top); Platt Saco Lowell, pages 15 (bottom) and 16 (bottom); Oldham Corporation, page 17 (top); Shiloh Spinners, page 17 (bottom); Oldham Chronicle, page 18 (top); Carrington Viyella, page 18 (bottom).

COVER: *Photograph reproduced by kind permission of Simon Midgley and the Queen Street Mill Textile Museum.*

BELOW: *An early method of untangling and cleaning cotton once it had been taken from the bale was 'batting' with sticks of hazel or holly. The cotton was laid on a surface of cords, which formed a kind of elastic grating, through which the impurities fell.*

Manchester mills and workers' houses in 1815. This engraving of the Ancoats district shows the start of unplanned urbanisation. The fields in the foreground were soon covered with buildings as the city grew at an astonishing rate.

THE RISE AND FALL OF
THE COTTON INDUSTRY

It will doubtless seem strange to future generations that Britain's supremacy during the nineteenth century depended to a large extent on a plant grown thousands of miles from her shores and on an industry which sprang up in one of the most isolated corners of the kingdom. Cotton was Britain's principal source of wealth; and in Lancashire, where the industry was concentrated, the mill owners boasted that they met the needs of the home market before breakfast and devoted the rest of the day to exports. In recent years the decline of the cotton industry has been almost as rapid as its furious growth two hundred years ago. Its legacy, however, is experienced by all who live in the industrial societies it helped to create.

Before the eastern half of Lancashire and the adjoining parts of Yorkshire and Cheshire were transformed into a region of almost three hundred factory towns and villages, they were the centre of a scattered home-based industry, which relied on London for its markets, capital and technical advancement. The weaving of fustians — cloth with a cotton weft and a linen warp — was introduced into East Anglia in the sixteenth century by settlers from the Low Countries and by 1600 had reached Lancashire. There it continued alongside the ancient woollen industry until the invention of mass-production machinery in the second half of the eighteenth century gave it a new impetus and provided one of the main starting points of the industrial revolution.

Lancashire proved to be the perfect setting for the expanding cotton trade. Even its inhospitable climate was an advantage. The damp Pennine air, by helping the fibres to cling together, reduced the strain placed on them by machinery: manufacturers who built mills in drier regions found that production costs were about ten per cent more. Land in Lan-

3

cashire was cheap; coal and soft water (essential for bleaching, dyeing and printing) were plentiful and the ease with which they could be obtained encouraged the introduction of steam power. Liverpool was an ideal port and Manchester an ideal market place for the compact region, which was untroubled by the restrictive practices of ancient corporations or guilds and which welcomed the opportunity to co-operate with foreigners.

By 1800 all the processes for making cotton goods in factories had been brought into use: what followed during the next hundred years was the perfection of basic ideas, in particular those concerned with weaving. The late eighteenth century also saw the introduction both of James Watt's rotary steam engine, which gradually replaced the horse capstan and the waterwheel as the industry's main power source, and (in America) of Eli Whitney's saw gin, which opened up the fertile cotton fields of the Southern States just as West Indian and other supplies were beginning to prove inadequate. The contribution of the American growers was very great: by increasing productivity, they were able consistently to reduce their prices until 1898. Mechanisation had sharply lowered the cost of yarn and manufactured goods before the benefits of Whitney's gin were felt; thereafter cheap American cotton enabled Lancashire to sell even to the poorest nations — by 1843 India was the largest customer — and to become the home of the first industry to make the whole world its market.

The cotton trade was largely created by self-made men during a period of spectacular growth lasting from 1770 to 1840; it continued to expand for another seventy years, reaching its peak in 1912, when 8,000 million yards (7,300 million metres) of cloth were produced. By 1803 cotton had overtaken wool as Britain's leading export, a position it retained until 1938, when machinery moved into first place. Sales of cotton yarn and goods in 1830 brought in just over half of Britain's overseas earnings; afterwards the percentage fell, but it was a third until the 1880s and a quarter until the First World War. There was a short-lived boom when the

war ended, but then began a decline which has been called 'the most terrible retreat in the history of industry'.

It was inevitable that a trade which imported all its raw material would sooner or later be harmed by events it was powerless to prevent. The cotton famine, caused by the American Civil War of 1861-4, emphasised this most forcibly. By that time other countries had already set up their own cotton industries. Lancashire had little to fear from Europe, but when cotton-growing and low-wage countries also became manufacturers, markets began to be lost. The restriction on the export of textile machinery was lifted in 1843: within ten years India had her own cotton mills; Brazil in the 1860s and Japan in the 1870s followed this lead. By 1880 half the world's cotton consumption was in new areas. Asia took less British yarn and then less cloth. In 1933 Japan, which introduced round-the-clock working thirty years before Lancashire, became the largest exporter of cotton goods.

While Lancashire retained the spinning mule, competitors installed the faster ringframe. They also avoided over-specialisation,which in Britain had put spinning, weaving and finishing in different hands. Complacency and a reluctance to change old methods contributed to cotton's decline. In 1930 the trade earned sixteen per cent of Britain's export revenue; by the 1950s the contribution was down to single figures, and in 1958 Britain became a net importer of cotton goods for the first time since the eighteenth century. In the following year Parliament passed the Cotton Industry Act, which compensated employers for getting rid of old machinery. More than twelve million spindles and nearly 105,000 looms were scrapped and the workforce fell in two years by thirty per cent. The government wished to see a streamlined industry, but modernisation and extra shift working were unable to stem its steady contraction. Cheap foreign cloth forced more mill closures, which averaged almost one a week during the 1960s and 1970s. The mills found new uses and by the early 1980s cotton in many parts of Lancashire was only a memory.

This engraving of an early nineteenth-century mill shows the process of willowing, which loosened and cleaned the raw cotton after it was taken from the bale. The machine consisted of a rapidly revolving drum covered with iron spikes. Dust was drawn through the pipe and the trash (dirt, seeds and husks) fell on to the floor.

PREPARING THE RAW COTTON

Cotton arrives at the mill in bales and has to be disentangled, cleaned, blended and turned into a slender rope of parallel fibres — the *roving* — before it can be spun into yarn. Until the introduction of machinery, raw cotton was beaten with sticks and combed between the metal teeth of hand cards to form a fleecy roll, which was then reduced to a roving on the spinning wheel. So long as cotton was carefully picked by hand and loosely baled it could be handled easily on receipt, but once the harvesting, ginning and baling were done mechanically new opening and cleaning methods became essential. Machines introduced towards the end of the eighteenth century established the principles used today. The revolving teeth of the *willow* and the beating action of the *scutcher* break up the tightly pressed cotton and free seeds, leaves, stalks and

dirt, known collectively as *trash*. No two bales of cotton are exactly alike and in order to obtain a uniform yarn a good mixing must be made. As many as a hundred bales are blended in some mills, but between twelve and twenty is a more usual number. The end product of the initial processing is a *lap* of matted tufts, which is fed into the carding engine.

Carding was among the first textile processes to be mechanised. As early as 1748 patents for cylinder machines were taken out by Daniel Bourne, of Leominster, and by Lewis Paul, of Birmingham, who also pioneered spinning by rollers, but it was not until 1775 that Richard Arkwright brought together the basic features of the modern carding engine. Earlier machines had to be stopped frequently to remove the cotton; by introducing a continuous doffing device, Arkwright made possible the application of power. The carding engine produces a continuous roll of cotton, but because of the interchange between the cylinder and the doffer the fibres are at all angles and need to be drawn out (drafted) to make them parallel. It was Arkwright again who provided the drawing and roving frames to prepare the cotton for the spinner. Extra machines were added in later years to refine the process, but modern systems have reduced their number. Precision engineering has enabled the speeds of preparation machinery to be increased enormously in recent years and further advantages have been derived from linking the machines into 'automated' systems.

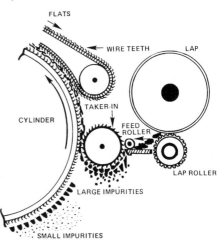

RIGHT: Carding takes place between surfaces covered with closely set needle-pointed wires. Carding removes impurities left in the cotton from previous processes and converts the lap into a loose rope of fibres known as a sliver. It is about 1 inch (25 mm) in diameter.

BELOW: This wooden carding engine was constructed at Arkwright's Cromford Mill in about 1775. Cotton fed into the back of the machine was reduced to a filmy web by the combing action of metal spikes on the revolving drum and on the underside of the ten 'flats' placed above it. The carded cotton was taken up by the smaller ('doffer') roller, from which it was removed by an oscillating comb. The web was then drawn through the rollers at the front of the machine in the form of a loose rope. Carding engines require millions of teeth. In Arkwright's day they were set in leather by children, who were paid a penny for every three thousand, a task which usually took about four hours.

ABOVE: *An idealised picture of a card room in the early 1830s. The artist has drawn the machines in admirable detail but has left out the haze of dust, which invariably surrounded them. 'Carder's cough' was a common complaint. On the right is a doubling machine.*
BELOW: *A modern card room. In the foreground are cans of sliver produced by the high-speed carding engines. Great attention is given to dust control in present-day factories. Waste is removed pneumatically through underfloor ducting.*

LEFT: *Spinning wheels like this were used for five hundred years until the machines of mass-production were invented in the eighteenth century. The principle of the Jersey wheel — spinning from the spindle tip — was used by Hargreaves in his jenny and Crompton in his mule. In the foreground are iron-toothed hand cards for untangling the raw cotton and drawing the fibres into parallel strands.*

RIGHT: *Spinning on the Jersey (cottage) wheel. The spinner attaches the roving to the spindle and draws it out with his left hand, at the same time adding a slight amount of twist for strength by turning the driving wheel with his right hand. When the thread has been fully drawn, the required twist is inserted by turning the driving wheel more rapidly. Spinning can take place only when the thread is held at an angle which allows it to slip off the spindle tip. After twist has been inserted, the spinner moves his left hand to a position at right angles to the spindle, which is then revolved for the winding.*

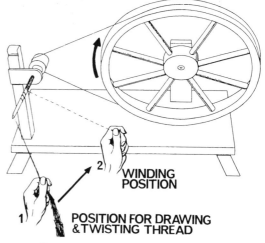

WINDING POSITION

POSITION FOR DRAWING & TWISTING THREAD

James Hargreaves's spinning jenny of 1764 used the principle of the Jersey wheel. The machine was far from perfect and could spin only sixteen threads at once; improved versions had as many as 120 spindles. At one point, Hargreaves required the spinner to use both hands and a foot, an operation calling for considerable agility. The girl in the photograph has stretched the threads with the drawbar and is about to turn the wheel to drive the spindles. After putting sufficient twist into the yarn, she uses her foot to control the faller wire, which guides the threads as they are wound evenly into cops. The machine was built at Helmshore in 1963 from Hargreaves's patent specification of 1770.

SPINNING

Spinning — the drawing out and twisting together of fibres to form a long thread — was done entirely by hand until the eighteenth century. Inventors then incorporated the principles of the two kinds of spinning wheel into machines of mass production. There was also a new idea: the attenuation of the roving by sets of rollers travelling at successively faster speeds. Rollers were first tried by Lewis Paul and

ABOVE: *Several inventors added improvements to Hargreaves's jenny. Most importantly, the horizontal driving wheel was replaced by a vertical one, thus making possible machines with as many spindles as one person could turn by hand: about a hundred was the average number. Jennies were used in domestic workshops and factories. Power was never applied to the jenny, which fell out of use in the cotton trade before the middle of the nineteenth century.*

LEFT: *Several kinds of jenny were made in the 1760s and 1770s. All were extensions of the Jersey spinning wheel. This machine was invented by Thomas Highs, a reedmaker of Leigh. Arkwright is believed to have derived the idea of roller spinning from Highs.*

John Wyatt, who met in Birmingham in 1732. Paul took out a patent in 1738 and the two men built a mill in the city three years later. This failed, but a larger water-driven mill in Northampton — it had five machines of fifty spindles — ran from 1743 until 1764. For the first time there was, in the words of the poet Dyer, 'a machine . . . which draws and spins the thread without the tedious task of needless hands'. The mill seems to have been poorly managed and the machine was far from perfect mechanically. The idea was also a little before its time: the demand for spun cotton was beginning to grow just as the enterprise was abandoned. By then James Hargreaves, a hand-loom weaver from Oswaldtwistle in Lancashire, was working on his jenny (the word means engine), which extended the spinning cycle of the Jersey wheel to eight spindles and in later models to more than one hundred. For a time the jenny was regarded with suspicion by those who feared it would throw them out of work and in 1768 a mob attacked the inventor's home and destroyed the frames of twenty machines he was building in a barn. Shortly afterwards, Hargreaves accepted an invitation to settle in Nottingham, where there was a strong demand for hosiery yarn and a readier appreciation of new ideas. (The stocking knitting frame had been invented by the Reverend William Lee as early as 1589.)

While Hargreaves was suffering at the hands of the rioters, Richard Arkwright, a barber turned wigmaker, was working only a few miles away at Preston on a spinning machine of a different kind. Helped by a clockmaker named Kay, he managed to spin four threads at once, drawing the threads with rollers and twisting them with flyers — a feature of both the Saxony spinning wheel and the Paul-Wyatt

A 96-spindle water-frame from Cromford Mill, Derbyshire. Like all Arkwright's original machinery, it was built in the mill by his own workmen. The framework is of wood, as is the large drum which transmitted the power from the waterwheel to the two halves of the machine. The roving from the bobbins at the top of the machine is drawn out by three pairs of rollers and then twisted by the flyers at the foot of the frame. No special skills were needed to operate machines like this. Changing the bobbins and joining broken threads were jobs frequently undertaken by young children.

machine. Arkwright also settled in Nottingham, choosing a site in the Hockley district only a short distance from the small jenny mill started by Hargreaves and his partner Thomas James.

Unlike the jenny, which needed three separate operations to spin and wind a length of yarn, Arkwright's frame had a continuous action and was eminently suitable for the application of power. The Nottingham mill used horses, but a second, built at Cromford, Derbyshire, in 1771, was driven by a waterwheel. The four-spindle prototype had by now grown into the water-frame, which spun a wiry yarn that was ideal for warps. With the jenny supplying the weft, the price of cotton goods fell sharply. By 1788 some twenty thousand jennies and 143 Arkwright-type mills were in use and the spinning wheel was virtually obsolete.

The revolution in spinning culminated in 1779 when Samuel Crompton, of Bolton, completed seven years' work on his mule, which was a combination of the jenny and the water-frame. It spun such fine yarns that British weavers were able to match the muslins of India. Like the jenny, the mule was a hand-operated machine with an intermittent action; making it semi-automatic and then 'self-acting' engaged the labours

Arkwright's water-frame underwent several improvements and in its more compact form was known as the throstle (above). It was widely used during the first half of the nineteenth century. The spinning principle remained the same, however. The diagram below shows the thread being drawn out by the three pairs of rollers before being twisted by the rotating arm of the flyer.

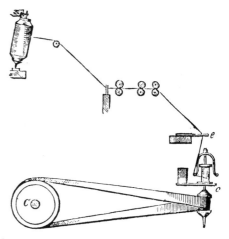

12

This mule, built in England in about 1790 and now on display in Ghent following restoration in 1978, is the only complete hand-driven machine to have survived. Samuel Crompton's first mule (1779) had forty-eight spindles. It is likely that the Ghent machine was given only thirty in order that it could be more easily smuggled to Belgium. The export of textile machinery was illegal from 1782 until 1843. However, machines did find their way out of Britain and were used to start cotton enterprises in many parts of Europe.

of many inventors. When trade unions were legalised in 1825, the mule spinners were the first group of workers to try to exploit their new freedom. This prompted the masters to commission Richard Roberts, a Manchester engineer who had improved the power-loom, to design a fully automatic mule. He succeeded brilliantly. As a writer of the time put it, 'the self-acting mule is one of the most beautiful specimens of mechanical combination that is to be found; it furnishes an illustrious example of the wonderful perfection to which machinery has attained in our manufacturing processes.' Crompton's first mule had forty-eight spindles; by 1800 machines with four hundred were in production; the 'self-acting' mule increased the number again until pairs with between two thousand and two thousand five hundred spindles were in common use.

While British inventors concentrated on refining the mule — it was more or less perfect by 1885 — their counterparts in the United States devoted their energies to the throstle, an improved version of Arkwright's water-frame, and produced in the late 1820s a series of devices which greatly advanced the cause of continuous spinning. After more than three hundred years, the flyer was replaced by a metal ring around which a loop called a 'traveller' was drawn by the thread. Ring spinning became immensely popular in America but was adopted only slowly in Britain: it was not until the 1950s that it became the predominant system.

The ringframe, which has been used for 150 years, is being seriously challenged by what are known as 'break' or 'open-end' machines. The principle on which they are based is not new: a Burnley inventor called Williams embodied the idea in a patent as long ago as 1807, but it was only

13

ABOVE: *An early mule factory with machines that required manual power as well as that trans-mitted from the overhead shafting. Until mules were made self-acting, the spinner moved the carriage by turning a driving wheel. Mule spinners employed their own assistants. The picture includes a piecer twisting together broken threads and a child picking up waste from underneath the frame.*

BELOW: *The self-acting mule was one of the most remarkable inventions of the nineteenth century. The mills of Lancashire once housed several thousand of these huge machines, which could spin the very finest of threads.*

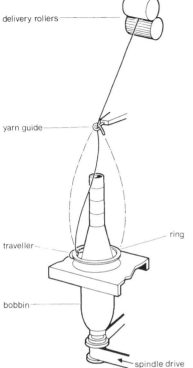

delivery rollers

yarn guide

traveller

bobbin

ring

spindle drive

during the 1970s that machines came into use. Twisting and winding are divorced, thus doing away with the need to rotate the yarn bobbin. The flow of fibres is broken, leaving a so-called 'open-end' to the yarn being made. The fibres travel separately across the break and attach themselves to the open-end of the yarn, which is twisted at very high speeds. Less power is needed and yarn packages can be made much larger than by conventional means.

LEFT: *Ring spinning replaced the mule as the leading method in Britain only in the 1950s. The ringframe, like Arkwright's water-frame, uses rollers to do the drafting. Twist is put into the yarn by the combined action of the spindle, ring and traveller. Yarn is threaded through the yarn guide and traveller (an almost oval piece of metal or plastic, which fits over the ring) on to the bobbin. The rotation of the spindle drags the traveller round the ring, each revolution inserting one turn of twist. The drag imposed by the ring causes the traveller to lag behind the spindle by an amount sufficient to wind the twisted yarn on to the bobbin.*

BELOW: *Ring spinning in a modern mill. This machine, built by Platt Saco Lowell, has 416 spindles working at between 12,000 and 13,000 rpm.*

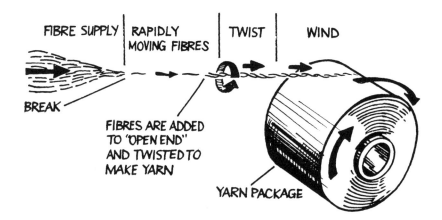

FIBRE SUPPLY | RAPIDLY MOVING FIBRES | TWIST | WIND

BREAK

FIBRES ARE ADDED TO "OPEN END" AND TWISTED TO MAKE YARN

YARN PACKAGE

ABOVE: 'Open-end' or 'break' spinning has greatly increased yarn output since its introduction in the mid 1960s, though the basic idea was suggested in the early nineteenth century. A break is made between the fibre supply and the twisted thread. Individual fibres are drawn across the gap and attach themselves to the 'open end' of the yarn. Because yarn is no longer wound on to a spindle bobbin, very large packages can be made at high speeds.

BELOW: 'Open-end' spinning in a modern mill. Arkwright would recognise the machine but would be astonished at the progress made. The water-frame had a speed of about 2,000 rpm; the latest open-end machines operate at 60,000 rpm. A plant such as this produces more yarn than the entire industry in the days of the spinning wheel.

ABOVE: *Cotton mills dominate the Lancashire landscape, especially in the spinning areas, but not until the 1860s did buildings of architectural merit appear. United Mill, built in 1874 at Chadderton, was a good example. It ceased production in 1959 and much of it has since been demolished.*
BELOW: *Elk Mill, Royton (1926), was the last of its kind to be built in the Oldham district; by then the cotton trade was in decline. Mule spinning continued at the mill until 1974. All the later spinning mills had short names: Ace, Ash, Bee, Era, Fox, Gem, Ivy, Oak, Orb, Owl, Ram, Roy, Sun and others. It cost less to paint a short name on returnable skips and cases and the letters could be made large.*

ABOVE: *The spinning town of Shaw, which once had the reputation of being the richest in England with more millionaires to the square mile than any other place on earth. Its mills, each with more than a hundred thousand spindles, were among the largest ever built. The boom began in Shaw in the 1870s, when suitable land in nearby Oldham was becoming scarce. Limited liability companies, most of which were promoted by working men, rapidly transformed the landscape. Some idea of the excitement of the times can be gained from this report of 1875: 'The other day a new company was announced at Shaw, and the day after the announcement was made, nearly 100 people from Oldham went by train to the scene... They rushed out of the carriages, knocked the ticket collector on one side, and threw their tickets on the ground. They then marched up the street at double quick, but finding this too slow, they set off in a run through the village and besieged the secretary in his house. The crowd was too great to be supplied at once and application forms for shares were soon selling at 6d and 1s each.... The shares are now selling at a premium.'*

BELOW: *Unit 1, opened at Atherton by Carrington Viyella in 1978, was the first completely new spinning mill to be built in Lancashire for fifty years. It cost £6 million and replaced an old mule spinning mill. Yarn from Unit 1 – 100,000 pounds (45,000 kg) weekly – was woven into sheets by another company in the CV group. Production ended in 1999 as the industry continued to contract.*

A hand-loom weaver. This old man is using a fly shuttle, the simple but revolutionary device invented by John Kay in 1733. By jerking the picking stick with his right hand, the weaver propels the shuttle across the loom by means of sliding hammers known as pickers. Before Kay's invention, the weaver had to use both hands to throw the shuttle backwards and forwards. Afterwards, his left hand was free to operate the batten, which is pulled forward after each throw to press the weft threads together. The photograph is of 'Owd Eccles', the last hand-loom weaver in Darwen.

WEAVING

During its early years, the cotton industry relied entirely on the wooden-framed hand-loom for its cloth; not until spinning had become a factory process did men attempt to bring about a similar change in weaving. The perfection of the power-loom, however, was a long process which taxed the ingenuity of numerous inventors. As early as 1774 Robert and Thomas Barber, of Bilborough in Nottinghamshire, took out a well conceived patent, but it was another ten years before the Reverend Edmund Cartwright designed the first power-loom ever built. Cartwright, who had many in-

ventions to his credit, stands apart from the other textile pioneers, since it was intellectual curiosity rather than a desire for money that stimulated his interest in weaving. Here is his own account of how the power-loom came to be invented: 'Happening to be at Matlock in the summer of 1784, I fell in company with some gentlemen of Manchester, when the conversation turned on Arkwright's spinning machinery. One of the company observed that as soon as Arkwright's patent expired so many mills would be erected and so much cotton spun that hands would never

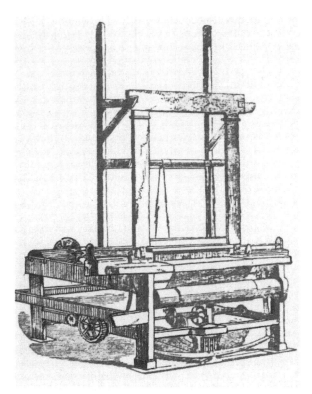

A power-loom of 1798, which had a speed of sixty picks (throws of the shuttle) a minute. This was no faster than a hand-loom and, since five weavers were needed to run six looms, the savings were small. Within fifty years, however, looms were working at 220 picks a minute.

be found to weave it. To this I replied that Arkwright must then set his wits to work to invent a weaving mill . . . The Manchester gentlemen unanimously agreed that the thing was impracticable; and in defence of their opinion they adduced arguments which I certainly was incompetent to answer or even to comprehend, being totally ignorant of the subject, having never at any time seen a person weave. I controverted, however, the impracticability of the thing by remarking that there had lately been exhibited in London an automaton figure which played at chess. "Now you will not assert, gentlemen," said I, "that it is more difficult to construct a machine that shall weave than one which shall make all the variety of moves that are required in that complicated game." '

Unaware that the automaton was controlled by hidden hands, Cartwright set out to prove his point. His loom did weave cloth but was, he admitted, 'a most rude piece of machinery'. Springs to propel the

shuttle were strong enough to send up a rocket and 'it required the strength of two powerful men to work the machine at a slow rate and only for a short time.' Nevertheless, it was a beginning. Cartwright patented his loom in 1785 and then 'condescended to see how other people wove'. He was astonished to find how far he still had to go and, much chastened, he returned to his drawing board. Cartwright was more satisfied with his second loom and went on to build a weaving shed at Doncaster in 1787. The power was supplied by a bull until a steam engine was installed two years later. Of the twenty looms, eighteen wove cotton. Financially, however, the venture was a failure and the shed closed in 1793. A Manchester manufacturer who bought twenty-four of Cartwright's machines in 1790 fared no better: hand-loom weavers burned down the factory.

Though concerted attacks were made on power-loom factories in 1812 and 1826,

ABOVE: *Though the power-loom was invented in 1785, it was still being developed when this engraving was made in about 1830. It shows the steam-driven weaving shed of Swainson, Birley and Company, near Preston. Each weaver ran two looms.*
BELOW: *The Lancashire loom was more or less perfected by 1850 and it remained popular even after the introduction of automatic weaving at the start of the twentieth century. The photograph of 1907 shows a Haslingden shed which housed a thousand tightly packed looms. When the mill closed in 1979, many had been running for more than a century. A number are preserved at the Quarry Bank Mill Museum at Styal in Cheshire.*

LEFT: *The manager of this mill at Helmshore is 'kissing' a shuttle — sucking the thread of a new cop through the eye. It was an unhygienic practice, but it was not until the mid 1950s that the use of hand-threaded shuttles became compulsory. Noise was another hazard in weaving sheds; the clatter of rows of closely packed looms affected the weavers' hearing. Lipreading was the only way of understanding a conversation.*

BELOW: *The weaving town of Burnley in 1912, when the cotton industry was at its peak. The scene, however, had changed little since 1870, by which time most of the town's 101 mills had been completed. The Leeds and Liverpool Canal in the centre of the photograph was the main supply route until the arrival of the railway in the 1840s.*

Luddism was not the main reason for the machine's slow progress. Far better looms than those invented by Cartwright and his immediate successors were needed to weave fault-free cloth at high speeds. The early looms, built at a time when engineering was in its infancy, had to be stopped every few minutes both to adjust the cloth and to 'dress' the warp threads as they unrolled from the beam. This required the weaver or his assistant to brush a flour paste on to the threads to give them enough strength to undergo the weaving. William Radcliffe, of Stockport, overcame this problem with his dressing machine of 1803. Other advances followed until, by the 1820s, it was generally agreed that the power-loom had come to stay. Another twenty years had to pass, however, before it included all the features of the Lancashir loom, which was universally used during the cotton trade's most successful years. William Dickinson's 'Blackburn loom' of 1828 introduced picking sticks to drive the shuttle backwards and forwards and in 1841 and 1842 Kenworthy and Bullough, also of Blackburn, completed the development era by patenting improvements, including a brake to stop the loom when the weft broke, which not only cut the weaver's labour by half but also improved the quality of the cloth. Operatives who had been able to run only two looms now took charge of four and sometimes six, even though the speeds were greater. When the Blackburn ironmaster Joseph Harrison began producing superbly engineered looms in the 1840s, it seemed that little more could be achieved, and as late as 1879 a leading authority on weaving observed: 'The early power-looms were heavy and clumsy, but Messrs Harrison made such great improvements that the looms exhibited at the Great Exhibition of 1851 have perhaps never been surpassed.' It was no uncommon thing for looms built after the middle of the century to be used for eighty and even a hundred years.

New devices continued to be brought forward, but, as one writer commented at the beginning of the twentieth century, 'Effort is more conspicuous than achievement. As it stands at present, the most efficient and most wonderful of looms is nothing more than a mass of complex mechanical parts, displaying fine ingenuity, but lacking in that automatic quality which accomplishes great results by simple means.' By then, however, the automatic loom was being developed in the United States and it was introduced into Britain in 1902. Its inventor, J. H. Northrop, having failed to interest English makers in his ideas, took out a United States patent in 1894. Its main feature was the automatic replenishment of weft. Previously, when a weft thread broke or the weft spool ran out, the weaver had to lift the shuttle from the loom, renew the spool and connect the weft. The Northrop loom had a new kind of shuttle, which was refilled by a rotating hopper. The weaver no longer handled the shuttle; he became a hopper filler able to look after twenty-four looms.

Improvements to the automatic loom have continued unabated. Since the Second World War science and technology have dominated development. The shuttle is becoming obsolete as weft is inserted by rapiers, grippers and air and water jets. The simultaneous insertion of a large number of weft threads to form a fabric is likely to be a feature of future weaving machines.

FINISHING THE CLOTH

The processes which give the desired finish to a piece of cloth have undergone numerous changes since the cotton industry began its rapid expansion in the late eighteenth century. Advances in chemistry and engineering have not only speeded up bleaching, dyeing and calico printing but have also led to the introduction of many new techniques.

At the start of the industrial revolution, all finishing methods were costly, primitive and slow. This was particularly true of bleaching, which required many acres of grassland for exposing the cloth to the action of sunlight and water. *Crofting* was alternated first with *bowking* — immersion in alkaline leys concocted from the ashes of trees and plants—and then with *souring* in buttermilk. The pieces were washed by hand in streams or in *becks* filled with running water. Eight months passed by before the operation was complete. The use

ABOVE: *Bleachfields, or crofts, were a familiar sight in the cotton districts both before and for some years after the discovery of chlorine in the late eighteenth century. This engraving was made near Glasgow in 1844. The women are spreading the pieces on the ground to be bleached by the action of the sun and water.*
BELOW: *This early works bleached yarn intended either for sewing cotton or for dyeing before being woven into coloured cloths such as checks and stripes. The picture shows an iron kier used for boiling caustic soda.*

A mid nineteenth-century dyehouse. The workman is passing the cloth through dye contained in a trough known as a beck. Workers in the finishing trades received government protection much later than their colleagues in other branches of the industry. A Royal Commission of 1855 found that many bleaching, dyeing and printing plants regularly worked fifteen and sixteen hours a day and often continued for several days and nights without stopping.

of dilute sulphuric acid for souring in the mid 1750s reduced the time by half, but the vital advance, which enabled the process to be completed in a few days, came at the end of the century when the power of chlorine to remove vegetable colours — first noticed by the French chemist Berthollet in 1785 — was made available in the form of bleaching powder (chloride of lime). New methods of mass-producing the bleacher's raw materials — soda ash, caustic soda and chlorine gas — were introduced during the nineteenth century, a period which also brought great improvements in machinery. Traditionally cloth was treated in bundles but, after the invention in 1828 of David Bentley's washing machine, the practice grew up of stitching the pieces together to form a continuous rope. In 1845 John Brooks, of the Sunnyside Print Works in Crawshawbooth, used steam power to carry the ropes of cloth through all the stages of the bleaching process.

Research laboratories were set up in the leading finishing works and, although secrets were well guarded, there was a useful exchange of scientific information, both at learned societies and at less formal meetings such as those arranged at Whalley in the early 1840s by Lyon Playfair. One who attended was John Mercer, of Clayton-le-Moors, the discoverer in 1850 of the means by which cotton through the action of strong caustic soda is given a lustre approaching that of silk.

Mercerisation was followed in 1856 by William Henry Perkin's discovery of the first artificial dye, mauve analine, which was extracted from coal tar, then a waste product from gasworks. The older method of dyeing involved up to nineteen different processes, including immersion in cow dung and water to remove superfluous metallic salts (mordants), with which cloth was treated in order to make a bond with the colouring matter. Since Perkin's day organic chemists have synthetised more than seven thousand dyes and pigments. In recent years very bright colours have been achieved with *reactive* dyestuffs, which become part of the fibre molecule and are therefore highly resistant to fading. It is now possible to fix dyes with radio waves, a method which greatly reduces the size of a conventional dyehouse.

Calico printing — a localised form of dyeing — has improved steadily since the introduction of Thomas Bell's cylinder machine in 1785. Automatic screen printing is also widely used today.

Cloth may be coated or combined with other materials to form protective clothing.

Charles Macintosh started the rainwear industry in Manchester as long ago as 1824, using naphtha from coal tar to dissolve rubber for his waterproof garments.

Modern science has produced a whole range of 'easy-care' finishes and we take for granted fabrics that do not shrink, need no ironing, resist creasing and are fireproof.

COTTON'S IMPACT
ON THE WORLD

Cotton's impact was enormous and far reaching, its most enduring memorial being the towns which sprang up following the widespread adoption of the standardised production methods the industry so successfully introduced. Once expansion began, Lancashire needed the skills not only of those directly concerned with the manufacture and marketing of cotton goods but also of engineers, builders, chemists, bankers, financiers and others. Their arrival speeded the transformation of Lancashire into a huge industrial region, which in turn attracted men and women of almost every trade and profession.

The demand for textile machinery, for steam engines and boilers, for mills and workers' houses, for gas (and later electric) lighting and for an efficient transport system concentrated Britain's best engineering skills in and around Manchester, which also became the home of engineering insurance, thus setting new standards for safety at work. The chemical industry of Merseyside and south Lancashire owes its origin to the cotton trade's heavy consumption of such items as dyestuffs, bleaching powder and soap. Mining, ironfounding, metalworking and glassmaking all expanded in response to cotton's demands. The Liverpool and Manchester Railway (1830), the first railway to be run with real professionalism, was soon followed by a network of lines, which covered the region, taking much of the traffic from the old turnpike roads and canals, which had themselves been built to service the budding industry. The Manchester Ship Canal (1894) brought ocean-going vessels to within easy reach of the mills; the city became a major port and the site (at Trafford Park) of the world's first and largest industrial estate.

The industry had an immense influence on the development of the American South and on other cotton-growing countries such as Egypt and India. Raw cotton was Britain's largest import from 1825 until 1873 and its movement over land and sea was made possible by specially constructed rail systems and shipping fleets. Among the diverse range of foreign products sent to Lancashire were such things as whale oil for lubrication, timber for building and buffalo hides for the skips which held the bobbins.

The cotton trade provided the ordinary people of many lands with their first opportunity to buy cheap and attractive clothing (in particular prints for women's dresses), drapery and sewing thread. New products and designs appeared regularly, leading to specialisation by individual firms and, indeed, whole towns. Spinning came to be concentrated in south Lancashire and weaving in the north. Rossendale, in the centre of the county, worked up waste from the rest of the industry. For many years the mills of Blackburn and Darwen wove almost exclusively for the Indian market, suffering severely when India imposed tariffs in the 1920s.

Because cotton combines easily with other fibres, it was soon used to make a growing number of mixed fabrics; it also took a share of its competitors' markets by imitating many of their traditional lines. Cotton sheets and handkerchiefs replaced those of linen; flannelette made inroads into the cheaper end of the woollen trade; velveteens and plushes, thanks to mercerisation, were given the look and feel of silk. During the twentieth century cotton began to face competition from man-made fibres. But being a natural rather than an oil-based product, it has a future that may grow brighter as the wells runs dry.

ABOVE: *The printing of cloth was greatly speeded by the introduction of power-driven machines in the late eighteenth century. Thomas Bell's first copper cylinder machine was built near Preston in 1785. Initially, the machines printed simple patterns, as in the 1830 engraving, or the outlines of complex designs which were completed on the block printers' tables. The early cylinder machine could print almost five hundred pieces a day, a block printer only six.*

BELOW: *A block printer at work. The old method is used for patterns with an exceptional number of colours or an unusually large 'repeat'. Some designs require more than a hundred different blocks. The printing surface is usually composed of metal strips set on edge in the wood. The printer positions the block with the help of pins which project from the corners and applies pressure with a maul. Photographed at the only British works where block printing is still carried on, at Stubbins.*

ABOVE: *Factory life as portrayed by Robert Cruickshank in 1832, the year in which Michael Sadler's select committee published its alarming 682-page report on the working conditions of children. Cruickshank produced a series of drawings, which unfavourably contrasted the lot of factory children with that of West Indian slaves.*

BELOW: *Victims of the cotton famine. This engraving of 1862 shows mill workers queuing for food at Mottram. The American Civil War, by greatly reducing the supply of cotton, caused widespread distress in the manufacturing districts. A wave of speculation on the Liverpool cotton exchange made prices soar and cotton was even taken from mills to be resold. Temporary schools and sewing classes were set up for the unemployed and the more able-bodied worked on town improvement schemes.*

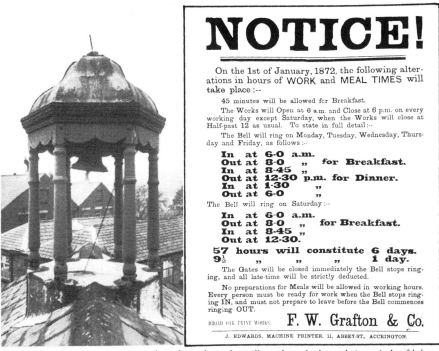

NOTICE!

On the 1st of January, 1872, the following alterations in hours of WORK and MEAL TIMES will take place :--

45 minutes will be allowed for Breakfast.

The Works will Open at 6 a.m. and Close at 6 p.m. on every working day except Saturday, when the Works will close at Half-past 12 as usual. To state in full detail :--

The Bell will ring on Monday, Tuesday, Wednesday, Thursday and Friday, as follows :--

In at 6·0 a.m.
Out at 8·0 ,, for Breakfast.
In at 8·45 ,,
Out at 12·30 p.m. for Dinner.
In at 1·30 ,,
Out at 6·0 ,,

The Bell will ring on Saturday :--

In at 6·0 a.m.
Out at 8·0 ,, for Breakfast.
In at 8·45 ,,
Out at 12·30.

57 hours will constitute 6 days.
9½ ,, ,, ,, 1 day.

The Gates will be closed immediately the Bell stops ringing, and all late-time will be strictly deducted.

No preparations for Meals will be allowed in working hours. Every person must be ready for work when the Bell stops ringing IN, and must not prepare to leave before the Bell commences ringing OUT.

BROAD OAK PRINT WORKS. **F. W. Grafton & Co.**

J. EDWARDS, MACHINE PRINTER, 11, ABBEY-ST., ACCRINGTON.

Bells and steam whistles summoned workpeople to the mills and marked out their periods of labour. The bell suspended above the Rosebank Printworks at Stubbins, near Ramsbottom, was attached to a chain which ran to the room below. It was last rung in 1974 after being used for 130 years. The notice of 1872 is from the Broad Oak Printworks at Accrington.

SOCIAL CONSEQUENCES

'Overwork', complained the French writer Léon Faucher in 1844, 'is a disease which Lancashire has inflicted upon England and which England in turn has inflicted upon Europe.' Work certainly dominated the lives of the cotton operatives, but though there was often far too much of it, it was regarded throughout the industry's years of growth as a virtue to be cultivated. There were two reasons for this: the spectacular success of indefatigable entrepreneurs like Arkwright and the first Robert Peel, and the teachings of equally successful religious leaders like John Wesley, the founder of Methodism, who went so far as to recommend child labour as a means of preventing youthful vice. The rapid accumulation of great wealth by working men and the ascent of the social ladder by the leading families in the trade — Peel's grandson became Prime Minister — gave

cotton an aura of romance, which cast its spell until the final decline set in. The industry was always an easy one to enter, though for every man who made his fortune there were many who failed (Samuel Crompton, inventor of the mule, among them). Here, however, is the story of one of the pioneers, written in 1837 by the factory inspector Leonard Horner: 'On Friday I went to Hyde, a large and densely populated village, and visited a very large mill belonging to a Mr Horsfield, a man nearly seventy years of age, who is said to be worth at least £300,000 and can hardly write his own name. I was very curious to hear from his own lips something of his history and so entered into conversation with him. He took me to his house hard by as he was going to dine. He had a piece of cold beef and potatoes; no wine. He keeps one woman servant. His daughter was not

29

much in appearance above the maid. He told me that at eighteen years of age he had not five shillings in the world beyond his weekly wages of fifteen shillings. Out of his wages he saved £28, bought a spinning jenny and made £30 the first year. In 1831 he made £24,000 of profit. He employs 1,200 people. He is not a solitary case; there are many not unlike him in this part of the country.'

The factory system, which was firmly established by men like Horsfield, has often been blamed for introducing long hours, the exploitation of children and bad working conditions. All these, however, had been the lot of domestic workers for generations; and the hand-loom weavers who chose to remain independent in the face of steam power had to work even harder than before for increasingly smaller wages. What was new about the factory system was the strict, irksome and often harsh discipline: the long lists of rules and their attendant fines; the peremptory summons of the factory bell; the payment of wages in the form of overpriced goods. Because the early factory masters expected their employees to put in as much time as themselves, they opposed attempts to reduce the hours of labour. The sufferings of young children, who were required to work twelve or fourteen hours a day and who were often beaten to keep them awake, aroused widespread indignation. With the government reluctant to intervene in business, it needed the prolonged efforts of a powerful humanitarian movement to achieve the legislation which curbed the worst excesses of the factory system and which set up a paid inspectorate in 1833 to ensure that the provisions of the Factory Acts were enforced. It was not until the passing of the Ten Hours Act in 1847 that workpeople had much time for recreation. Moses Heap, a Rossendale spinner, noted in his diary: 'For a while we did not know how to pass our time away. Before, it had been all bed and work; now, in place of seventy hours a week, we had fifty-five and a half. It became a practice, mostly on Saturdays, to play football and cricket, which had never been done before.'

When that was written, it was still possible to find in Lancashire a dwindling number of hand-loom weavers. For the most part, however, the world's first in-dustrial society was composed of what Karl Marx called 'new-fangled men, who are as much a part of modern times as machinery itself'. As early as 1823 Richard Guest, one of the cotton trade's first historians, had observed: 'Workmen being thrown together in great numbers had their faculties sharpened and improved by constant communication . . . During the last forty years the mind of the labouring class has been progressively improving and within the last twenty has made an advance of centuries and is still advancing with accelerated rapidity.'

Working conditions, however, did not improve at the same rapid rate. Cotton mills were noisy, dusty and in the early days of the industry decidedly dangerous. There were some notable exceptions like those at Barrowbridge and Eagley on the outskirts of Bolton. The first, which was visited by Prince Albert in 1851, was described by the *Illustrated London News* as 'a well organised community never equalled in the Utopias of philosophy'. Newspapers and periodicals were provided in a well heated reading room; there was a spacious dining area, a lecture hall, a co-operative store and substantial houses with gardens which were let to the workers at modest rents. Eagley had similar attractions together with shower baths, a library, evening classes and a park 'interspersed with seats and arbours'.

One mill — Cheesden Pasture on the high moors above Heywood — had its own pulpit. On Sundays the warehouse became a chapel, and once a year it was the setting for the Cheesden Tea and Oratorio, the oratorio always being Handel's *Messiah*. The singers and the small orchestra were all workers at the mill, and for the oratorio they borrowed a harmonium which they carried across the moor on two mop handles. The story tells us much about the cotton workers of the mid nineteenth century, not least their ability to overcome extreme difficulties.

The following description of a Littleborough weaving shed, 'neither the best nor the worst of its class', was written in the 1880s: 'It was filled with ordinary Lancashire looms, with both men and women running three or four each. The looms were so closely packed together that the weaver had very little room to pass between them. All sweeping, cleaning and oiling was done by the weavers, who also had to pull the cuts off the roller and fetch their own weft. Very little provision was made in winter for heating the shed or in summer for cooling it. Many times in midwinter the temperature was at freezing point, and when steaming was introduced to make the warps weave better, the condensed moisture dropped all over the place. In summer watering cans were employed to moisten the floor to keep the atmosphere humid. Provisions for the comfort of the workpeople were meagre. The only way to warm meals was to place them on the boiler; and at meal times the weavers could either eat their food in the boiler house among the coal dust or stop in the cold weaving shed. The only place for drying clothes was again the friendly boiler house — if you got the chance. The mill was lit with gas and when it had to be kept burning — as happened many times during the winter — for whole days together, the carbon dioxide nearly knocked you down when you went in.'

The cotton unions gradually achieved improvements, but a number of mills which were built in the early days of the industry have remained in use until the present, and modernisation has been exceedingly difficult. Some later mills, however, were altogether different and many owed their superiority to the workers who built them. The urbanisation of the cotton districts gave rise to an astonishing number of political, religious, educational and social movements, in which the working classes took an active and often a leading part. This experience fitted them well for mill management, for which the Co-operative Movement of the 1840s and 1850s provided the example and inspiration.

So successful were several of the co-operative mills of Rossendale — the Bacup and Wardle Commercial Company, founded in 1850, paid dividends as high as sixty-two per cent — that the district became known as the Golden Valley. The Joint Stock Acts of 1855 and 1862 helped the trend, which culminated in an astonishing

building boom at Oldham. The new entrepreneurs, who raised much of their initial capital by holding tea parties and dances and by canvassing their neighbours, succeeded in turning the town into the world's most important spinning centre with more spindles than the United States and France. Some seventy limited companies were registered between 1873 and 1875 alone and, according to the *Co-operative News*, 'Three-fourths at least of the shareholders are *bona fide* working men. Hundreds of cases could be instanced in Oldham of working men, in receipt of £1 or £1 10s a week, who have their hundreds of pounds in these companies.'

Karl Marx's 'new-fangled men' had become enthusiastic small capitalists, whose share dealings led to the formation of the Oldham Stock Exchange and required the services of forty brokers.

'What most filled the eye in the Lancashire of the nineties', wrote B. Bowker in *Lancashire under the Hammer*, 'was the efficiency of both master and man . . . Lancashire was an astonishing place. It had a cotton-making machine — compact, efficient, established — without real rival. The day of easy money was at hand.' The years 1900 to 1914 were described by Bowker as the 'gold rush', when 'any man who could tell or be taught the difference between healds and reeds, who could rake together a few hundreds of capital and rent some room and power was "made". ' And he added: 'With ordinary care for a dozen years, he would be able to retire to a mansion at Southport or a villa on the Blackpool coast. Indeed, with the barest trifle more than usual luck, he might meet his ambition half way by living at St Annes and being borne godlike each day to Manchester on a "club" express, which no ordinary mortal might enter.'

It would have seemed inconceivable to these men that disaster was at hand, but in the early 1920s came the slump which marked the start of the long and savage decline of Britain's greatest — and, in retrospect, most unlikely — industry.

FURTHER READING

Aspin, Chris. *The Water-Spinners*. Helmshore Local History Society, 2003.
Calladine, Anthony, and Fricker, Jean. *East Cheshire Textile Mills*. RCHNE, 1993.
Giles, Colum, and Goodhall, Ian H. *Yorkshire Textile Mills 1770-1830*. HMSO, 1992.
Industrial Archaeology Review, volume XVI, autumn 1993. This volume is devoted to textile mills.
Ingle, George. *Yorkshire Cotton*. Carnegie Publishing, 1997.
Rose, Mary B. (editor). *The Lancashire Cotton Industry*. Lancashire County Books, 1995.
Williams, Mike, with Farnie, D.A. *Cotton Mills in Greater Manchester*. Carnegie Publishing, 1992.

PLACES TO VISIT

Between Manchester and Oldham huge brick spinning mills dominate the landscape. Some of the biggest mills built may be seen at Shaw, while there are others in Bolton and Leigh. India Mill at Darwen has a chimney built in the 1860s in the style of an Italian tower. Near the mill an old steam engine is preserved in the open air. An older beam engine can be seen in Bolton town centre. The museums listed here contain machinery or other items connected with the cotton industry. Intending visitors are advised to find out the times of opening before making a special journey. (See also www.spinningtheweb.org.uk)

Blackburn Museum and Art Gallery, Museum Street, Blackburn, Lancashire BB1 7AJ. Telephone: 01254 667130. Website: www.blackburn.gov.uk Includes reproductions of spinning jenny and mule, together with hand-looms, power-looms, etc.

Clitheroe Castle Museum, Castle Hill, Clitheroe, Lancashire BB7 1BA. Telephone: 01200 424568. Website: www.ribblevalley.gov.uk

Cromford Mill, Mill Lane, Cromford, Derbyshire DE4 3RQ. Telephone: 01629 824297 (Arkwright Society). Website: www.arkwrightsociety.org.uk Mill built by Arkwright; has exhibitions on spinning and weaving.

Derwent Valley Visitor Centre, Belper North Mill, Bridgefoot, Belper, Derbyshire DE56 1YD. Telephone: 01773 880474. Website: www.belpernorthmill.org The centre is housed in the cotton mill built in 1803 by William Strutt.

Helmshore Mills Textile Museum, Holcombe Road, Helmshore, Rossendale, Lancashire BB4 4NP. Telephone: 01706 226459. Website: www.lancashire.gov.uk Spinning mules can be seen at work in this old cotton mill. The museum has the only complete Arkwright water frame in the world and other Arkwright machinery. There is also a display gallery, and ancillary industries are also covered.

Museum of Science and Industry in Manchester, Liverpool Road, Castlefield, Manchester M3 4FP. Telephone: 0161 832 2244. Website: www.mosi.org.uk Displays include textile manufacture and three great mill engines.

Quarry Bank Mill, Styal, Wilmslow, Cheshire SK9 4LA. Telephone: 01625 445896. Website: www.quarrybankmill.org.uk The power-loom room and weaving shed of this 200-year-old cotton mill are run by the National Trust as a working museum; there are also hand spinning and weaving demonstrations, galleries on the history of the industry, and the preserved workers' village of Styal.

Queen Street Mill Textile Museum, Harle Syke, Burnley BB10 2HX. Telephone: 01282 412555. Website: www.lancashire.gov.uk

Science Museum, Exhibition Road, South Kensington, London SW7 2DD. Telephone: 0870 870 4868. Website: www.sciencemuseum.org.uk Exhibits include Arkwright's first spinning frame, machines from Cromford and a power-loom exhibited by Joseph Harrison at the Great Exhibition.

Sir Richard Arkwright's Masson Mills Working Textile Museum, Derby Road, Matlock Bath, Derbyshire DE4 3PY. Telephone: 01629 581001. Website: www.massonmills.co.uk

Towneley Hall Art Gallery and Museums, Towneley Hall, Towneley Park, Burnley, Lancashire BB11 3RQ. Telephone: 01282 424213. Website: www.towneleyhall.org.uk